Praise for Billy Collins
and *Musical Tables*

"In [Billy] Collins's new book of very short poems, called *Musical Tables*, one named 'Oxymorons' lists 'beach culture,' 'happy birthday,' and 'family fun.' It's that dry humor which has helped make him a best-selling poet—another oxymoron."

—*The New Yorker*

"What makes Collins 'the most popular poet in America,' as he has been dubbed by *The New York Times*, is his signature mix of dry humor, perceptive observations, and accessibility, punctuated by constant surprises. In *Musical Tables*, Collins presents 125 short poems [with] just enough text to convey a mystery, question, or discovery. The brevity of the poems will remind some readers of their earliest encounters with poetry, when surprising visuals and phrasing made the genre seem almost magical."

—*Christian Science Monitor*

"Collins has said that the short poem is a sort of test for a poet: just as an artist should be able to draw a simple chicken, the poet should be able to channel meaning, emotion, profundity, and humor all through a couple of lines. Perhaps Collins is also aware of society's rapidly diminishing attention span, but he has created an undaunting, readable book of poetry that will appeal to all ages and hit you where it hurts."

—*LitHub*

"Collins's short poems warm the soul. Like koans and haiku, these micro-lyrics roam a range of tone and feeling, from elegies to epiphanies to bone-dry witticisms. . . . His formal compression is deft; his insights, arresting."

—*Oprah Daily*

"Billy Collins, a former poet laureate of the United States, is a real gem. He's a poet whose writing manages to be accessible, poignant and funny at the same time."

—*The Palm Beach Post*

"Tiny, tempting little poems."

—*The Community Library*

Also by Billy Collins

Sailing Alone Around the Room

Nine Horses

The Trouble with Poetry

Ballistics

Horoscopes for the Dead

Aimless Love

The Rain in Portugal

Whale Day

Edited by Billy Collins

Bright Wings

Poetry 180

180 More

Musical Tables

Musical Tables

Poems

BILLY COLLINS

RANDOM HOUSE

NEW YORK

2023 Random House Trade Paperback Edition

Copyright © 2022 by Billy Collins

Published in the United States by Random House, an imprint
and division of Penguin Random House LLC, New York.

RANDOM HOUSE and the HOUSE colophon are registered
trademarks of Penguin Random House LLC.

Originally published in hardcover in the United States
by Random House, an imprint and division of
Penguin Random House LLC, in 2022.

LIBRARY OF CONGRESS CATALOGING-IN-PUBLICATION DATA
Names: Collins, Billy, author.
Title: Musical tables : poems / Billy Collins.
Description: First Edition. | New York : Random House, [2022]
Identifiers: LCCN 2021057220 (print) | LCCN 2021057221 (ebook) |
ISBN 9780399589805 (paperback) | ISBN 9780399589799 (ebook)
Subjects: LCGFT: Poetry.
Classification: LCC PS3553.O47478 M87 2022 (print) |
LCC PS3553.O47478 (ebook) | DDC 811/.54—dc23
LC record available at https://lccn.loc.gov/2021057220
LC ebook record available at https://lccn.loc.gov/2021057221

Printed in the United States of America on acid-free paper

randomhousebooks.com

2 4 6 8 9 7 5 3 1

Book design by Dana Leigh Blanchette

for Steven and Eliza

for setting the stage again and again

". . . the face of the dog when she's chewing a carrot."

—NICK LAIRD

Contents

One

Two

Three

Four

Plus . . .

Musical Tables

Musical Tables

No one knew what to do
when the music stopped,
plus, the big tables were always in the way.

But soon it became the new game
in spite of its pointlessness,
or was that the reason for its popular appeal?

One

Highway

Hitchhiking alone,
I notice an ant
walking in the opposite direction.

Aa

At school,
always seen together,
capital and small,
parent and child

holding hands,
about to cross
the street
in Alphabet City.

The Naked Eye

There was no eye lid
to cover the naked eye

so she covered herself
with some scenery,

a meadow she liked to look at
when the other eye wasn't looking.

Argument from Design

Six petals on each iris,
every other one
with a small yellow streak,

which resembles a tiny vase,
holding a few flowers of its own.

New Calendar

The poem of next year—
every week a line,
every month a stanza,

and a tiny sun
rising and setting
in every numbered square.

The Mohawk Diner, 3 AM

Has that revolving cake stand
always been there

or did some men install it

while you and I sat here
at the counter not saying anything?

Dog

When she runs in her sleep,
eyelids twitching,
legs churning sideways on the floor,

I wonder if she's chasing
a squirrel or being chased
by an angry farmer waving a rake.

An Exaltation of Frogs

I know it's supposed to be larks,
but their full-throated croaking
early this rainy morning
after a night of more rain
is lifting me slightly off the floor.

Look

The morning lake
was smooth as a mirror.

A few angels were even seen
flying down

just after dawn
to check themselves out.

Limits

Even on a calm day
if you remain quiet
and hold your breath,

you still will not
be able to hear
the singing of the clouds.

Last to Leave the Party

In your white dress
you revolved around me
like the moon

and like the earth
I was spinning,
tilted back on my own axis.

The Dead of Winter

We will all die
in one month or another.

Many of the above
left us in December

while others will stay on
to see in the new year.

Carbon Dating

He tried it once
as a last resort

but most of the women
were a million years old.

From a Railing

A long barge
with a helpful
tugboat alongside

pushing parts
of the East River away
on their way somewhere.

Flaubert

As he looked for the right word,
several wrong words
appeared in his window.

Mute Potato

Before introducing it to a pot
of boiling water,

I caught a medium-size
Idaho potato

staring up at me
with several of its many eyes.

Headstones

If the dates show
the husband died
shortly after the wife—

first Gladys then Harry,
Betty followed by Tom—

the cause is often
gradual starvation
and not a broken heart.

Creative Writing

When I told a student
not to use single quotation marks
around lines of dialogue,

he told me that all our words
are already inside the quotation marks
that God placed around Creation.

The Code of the West

Say what you want
about me,
but leave the horse
I rode in on out of it.

Breaking Up

Like the nomadic dollar
I pass to the cashier

behind the register
you are off to other hands.

The Sociologist

I wandered lonely as a crowd.

Pupil

A hole in the eye,
the black well in the middle
of a flower, an iris,

or she who gives you the eye
sidelong on her way
out of the classroom, after the others.

Reflections on an Amish Childhood

I was a little square
in a round hat.

Night Sky

Lying on the beach
after so much wine and talk—
dippers everywhere.

Used Book

I turn a page
someone dog-eared,

like the bent ear
of a dog who's still lost.

Thelonious Morning

The breeze was slight
and moved only three

of the six wind chimes,
which formed a minor chord.

Seashore

A banded
Piping Plover

puts its best foot forward
then the other.

Random

Tossing a dart
at an open encyclopedia,
I happen to hit a flying squirrel.

Their kind, the entry explains,
as I close in,
are seldom seen

due to their nocturnal habits
and high dwelling places.
So much there to admire!

Teenager

Even a branch on an evergreen
may take an unexpected turn
up, down, or sideways

and grow substantial
in some weird direction.

Twisting Time

I am twisting again
but not like I did last summer
or the summer before
or the summer before that.

I am twisting more slowly now
because it is cold
and I have grown heavy
and there is hardly any wind.

D Major

A favorite
key signature
of pals

featuring,
as it does,
two sharps.

Simplicity

Dalmatian
is hard
to pronounce,

so the children,
pointing, say
fire truck dog.

Henry Wadsworth Longfellow

Trouble
was not
his middle name.

Eyes

O little twin spheres
echoing
the shape of the earth

and a perfect match
for the blue
curvature of the sky,

no wonder
the dark, descending birds
always begin with you.

Falling Asleep

Walking backwards
into a dark forest,

I sweep my footprints
out of existence

with a large
weightless branch.

A Memory

It came back to me
not in the way
a thing might be returned
to its rightful owner

but like dance music
traveling in the dark
from one end
of a lake to the other.

Poetry

As if it were not hard enough,
whenever my pencil

moves along the page,
the pink eraser end points up,

a little finger wagging,
reminding me of our appointment.

Two

Motel Parking Lot

Saying goodbye is so sad,
I don't even bother

to turn around to see
what it was you just threw at me.

View

In the summer sky
a cloud with its mouth open
eats a smaller cloud.

Flash

As my train
sped by a schoolyard,
I caught a tall boy
missing a basket.

The Visit

The wind blew
open the front door

and sat down
in my father's chair.

The Sunday Times

There's so much
going on in the world
besides these sausages.

The First Straw

The camel felt nothing
as it stood outside the tent,
its nose lifted in the thin desert air.

Koan in the Rain

You want to know
the sound of one hand clapping?

It is the same
as the sound of the other hand

holding the umbrella,
only slightly louder.

Crèche

For a moment,
the ox and a sheep
looked over at each other,

then they turned away
and went back
to adoring the Child.

ENG 243: The History of Egotism

You will notice, class,
that Wordsworth did not write

"Edward, the butcher's son,
wandered lonely as a cloud."

Hotel Room

Unlike
the breakfast menu,

I had no desire
to be hung

outside
before 2 am.

New York Directions

It's down
in the Village
between
Bleek
and Bleekest.

A Small Hotel

When a match touched
the edge of the page,
my poem filled with smoke,

then a few words
were seen to stumble out
in nothing but their nightgowns

with no idea which way to run.

Angelus

Church bells
from across the water—
a breeze blows
the letter I was reading
into the lake.

Physical

The nurse quipped
my pulse was so slow
she could take it with a sundial.

In a garden,
she watches the shadow move
while I sit there, ticking away.

4'33" by John Cage

As I listened,
the scales
fell from my eyes.

Olden Plea

Could we skip the hanging
and the quartering
and just do some drawings—
maybe of a pillory, an urchin, or a herring?

Three for a Quarter

Just as you can tell the age of a tree
by the rings within it,

you can tell the vintage
of a country song

by the coin required
to play a tune on the jukebox.

Yamaha

I gun my baby grand
along blacktop roads,

and I play *Clair de Lune*
in my helmet and boots.

Quatrain

When a woman
in a low-cut blouse
walked by,

the grocer in the doorway
raised his eyebrows
revealing the four lines in his forehead.

Dogma

I might be an atheist
were it not
for all the tall angels
and the pudgy cherubs
in the silvery clouds
presiding over all those miracles.

November Morning

My appearance at the shore
has surprised this pair of wood ducks—
the wild-haired male, the smooth-headed hen.

They've left the cover of reeds
to begin their day together,
and I have an afternoon flight to Milwaukee.

Google Maps

My parents' grave
is 1198 miles north of here.

17 hours and 23 minutes
from now,
I'll make believe I'm there.

Oxymorons

Family Fun

Beach Culture

Office Party

Dog Person

Children's Hospital

Light Pollution

Happy Birthday

Art Revolutionaries

Pollock, yes,
but let's not forget
whoever it was
that painted the first
still life without fruit.

Medium and Message

If John Keats
had ever held in his hand
a photograph of Marilyn Monroe,
his mind would have been blown twice, at once.

The Milky Way

A mother's face
hidden in the night sky,
stars clustered at her breasts.

In the morning
I pour her over cereal
with a scattering of berries.

Envelope

When a stamp was affixed
to the northeast corner,

all went dark
in the great state of Maine.

Jazz Man

I've taken some lessons
and worked on
some nice voicings for the chords

but all I have to do
is raise the keyboard cover one inch
and the cat dashes from the room.

Child Astronomy

After many hours
of peering
into a telescope

Goldilocks
discovers a dipper
that is just right.

Children

There's a new movie out
titled *Children*.

I don't know
what it's about

but I like the voice
on the radio

when it says:
"*Children*: now playing everywhere."

Three

Breakfast

In the hotel restaurant,
orange koi in a pond.
I toss in some corn flakes.

Divorce

No more heavy ball,
just the sound

of the dragged chain
with every other step.

Face Up

The jack of diamonds
lying supine
on the table,

a prince sleeping
in a pasture—
fifty-one cows.

Octopus Sonneteer

He wrote the octave
all at once

then dashed off the final six
while uncorking a bottle of champagne.

Dictionary Wanderings

The two silent "els"
in talk and calf

found a place
of prominence in llama.

Junior Philosopher

I'll have this figured out in no time,
he announced,
as he faced the Cosmic Void.
He was wearing
a clean white shirt
and holding
the tool kit of reason
by its handy leather strap.

Zen Backfire

The only time
I cut myself shaving

is when I'm aware
that I'm shaving.

Tom Thumb's Thumb

was so small
it failed to get the attention
of passing cars and trucks.

And what was he doing
out there anyway,
hitchhiking all by himself?

Neighborhood

What do I care
that they're tearing down
the nice old houses
and putting up brutal ones?

Before very long,
I'll be just a breeze
blowing around town,
trying to avoid all the wind chimes.

Wet Morning

The big red bougainvillea
is drooping,
an effect of last night's
wind and rain.

Thunder too,
but plants don't have ears,
or is that
what the petals are for?

Covid

Another long day
at home.

I set my phone
on Airplane Mode.

Empty House

After the old man died
but before the house was torn down,

the windows continued to enjoy
a view of the meadow and the woods beyond.

View from a Bridge

I never thought
of myself
as a little universe
inside a big one
until just now.

Spacing

When the traffic
in Los Angeles thickens
and comes to a stop,
the drivers in the other cars

look like they are pretending
to be from earth,
and not from some other planet
where this kind of thing never occurs.

Poetry Collection

They mutter
in the alleys of the city,

the old ones
who were not selected.

Orphans

Earth and moon
pulled through space,
a boy and his pale sister
forever spinning in a darkened room.

Departure

I wonder—
did you happen
to play something new
on the piano

just before you left

or was it the breeze
from the door
you left open
that turned the page?

Deep Mexican Night

You can hear them playing jai-alai
from this flowering terrace,

the distant rebounding ball,
and the fans with their strange cheer:
"Jai-alai-aiiahh-jaih-jaaiihaahaha!"

Charmed

The tiny figures
on your bracelet
ride around one wrist

while on the other
the hours
circle your pulse.

Celtic Interlacing

Early horizontal designs
for the rollercoasters of the future.

Corridor

I've grown old—
now my own name
rings a bell.

Deer Hit

The morning after
the tawny blur
in the windshield,

a sunny breeze
is stirring the woods
as I regard the damage—

a crumpled fender,
and one headlight
with an eyelash of fur.

Awake

Dead quiet night—
I lie in bed

waiting for
the other pin to drop.

Page-Turner

Desirable
in fiction.

Not so much
with a slim book of poems.

Pianissimo

At first,
I thought it meant
a really big piano.

Card Sharp

He said
he was born,
raised,
and re-raised
somewhere in Nevada.

Carpe Diem

As the coffee was brewing,
I learned from a book
that the trunks of elephants
are sensitive enough
to pick up a coin
and powerful enough to smash
a tiger to the ground,
and that was more than
enough seizing the day for me.

Italian Palindrome

A man.
A plan.
A canal.
Canaletto!

Avoidance

When I saw him
walking toward me in the city,
I stopped and looked in the window
of a store that had closed.

Turned out, it was only
someone who looked like him,
but all the way home, I wondered
where in the world he could possibly be.

Nurse

The one who spoke by a window
in a stairwell,
resting her head on her arm,
said she was so many stumbles
beyond tired,
she caught herself
envying the dead
for looking like sleepers in their beds.

Four

Refrigerator Light

The minute
she slams the door

I stop
thinking about her.

Summer

The two of us
one night in lawn chairs,
music coming from somewhere.

You explained
what we were hearing
was the B-side of the moon.

Morning Walk

The dog stops often
to sniff the poems of others
before reciting her own.

3:00 AM

Only my hand
is asleep,
but it's a start.

Poems

Because words
move from left to right,

the three fish
in the print on the wall,

who are facing the other way,
appear to be swimming upstream.

Saying

Two birds,
wings flapping
in a puddle of fresh rainwater.

Why kill them,
I wondered,
with one or even many stones?

Angler

Alone
with my thoughts

I spent the day
in the stream
of consciousness.

Corn Field

Far from any lake,
I walk in over my head.

A Rake's Progress

An autumn afternoon,
the neighbor's boy at work,

a pile of red and yellow
leaves growing ever higher.

Sunday Morning

Opening a book of poems
about flowers,

the cat amuses herself
while she waits for me to wake up.

The Student

She made asterisks
next to passages she liked,

little stars that kept shining
after she closed the book.

The English Professor

When I asked him
if he was in love,

he accused me
of anthropomorphizing him.

Fay

never amounted
to a hurricane,

just a lot of rain
with a girl's name.

Young Webster

After he spied her
in a garden
holding a rose parasol,

he defined *love* as
"something of
or pertaining to me."

Birthday Poem

Remember that birthday poem
I wrote for you?
It just stopped being about you.

After the Concert

It's so quiet now—
standing in the kitchen,
I can hear myself think.

Light-Year

Being the amount of light
that falls every year
on this green pasture

where I pulled the car over
to write down
what I just thought of.

Cornish

Would someone
please translate
her long memoir

into a language
almost no one speaks
or understands anymore?

Symphony No. 4 (Brahms)

The kettle drummer
fell asleep

while the triangle player
counted out his rests.

Reclining on Clouds

I would pray for you
but the gods would know
I was talking
to myself
and would turn
their curly
golden heads
the other way.

The Exception

Whoever said
there's a poem
lurking in the darkness
of every pencil
was not thinking of this one.

Quickie Ekphrasis

I looked at a postcard
of Mount Rushmore
while I cooled my tea with a spoon

then I turned over
the postcard of Mount Rushmore
and bit into a buttered scone.

Medieval Photography

Nothing came out very well.
People thought sitting still was odd.
Black and white had yet to be conceived,
even though many days were grey
with low clouds and unpredictable rain.
You remembered someone by closing your eyes.

Bad Hotel

I told the woman
from housekeeping,
who was eager to do my room,

to just come in
and pretend I'm not here,

which is exactly
what I had been doing
ever since I checked in.

Siren

So enchanting was her singing,
I turned the boat around

and tied her to my mast
so as to enjoy her melodies
as I sailed around this fascinating world.

Halloween

When I said hello
to a very small cowboy,
he gave me the trigger finger.

Elegy

I have turned over
all 52 cards
on the kitchen table.

Still, I think
you must be hiding
somewhere in the deck.

Disappointing Freak Show

A bearded man,
a one-headed chicken,
a sailor with a tattoo,
and a three-legged piano.

Coincidence

Along Came Betty
and
In Walked Bud.

Lazy Creator

And on the second day
he rested.

Weekday

Pure sunlight
on the miniature orange tree
and the white columns of the porch.

How extraordinary it would be
some morning on earth
to be dipped into creation.

Plus . . .

Card Table

After father says
game time is over,
it goes under the stairs,
its four legs folded up
like a giraffe saying its prayers.

Transitive Death

It's the bucket
that you kick when you kick,
but what is it
that you pass when you pass?

Music

I carried a tune
all the way to your doorstep
where it waited
for you to get home from work.

Narcissism

I want you to live
every moment
as if it were my last.

Early Tattoo

In blue ink
I drew
what was meant
to look like a tank
on my 5th grade arm
where a bicep
was meant to be.

Small Audience

Before movable type,
a poem would be written by hand.
Someone would read it alone
then hide it under her pillow.

Precocious

When I repeated
"There, there . . ."
my sobbing daughter
accused me
of quoting Gertrude Stein.

Simile

A poem about music
is like a branch about a bird.

The Children's Table

The peas
and dinner rolls
were flying in all directions
and one little boy
was up to his wrist
in the mashed potatoes.

Supine

A large airliner
passed overhead
flapping its silver wings.

As Time Goes By

Like the dog who forgot
where he buried a bone,
the old farmer forgot
where he buried the dog.

Afterword

When did my fascination with small poems begin? Maybe with nursery rhymes, but surely by high school when I was introduced to haiku. Later, I started finding them in the work of some of my favorite living poets, like Gary Snyder, Ron Padgett, Kay Ryan, and recently Charles Simic. I loved the suddenness of small poems. They seemed to arrive and depart at the same time, disappearing in a wink.

These days, whenever I pick up a new book of poems, I flip through the pages looking for small ones. Just as I might trust an abstract painter more if I knew he or she could draw a credible chicken, I have faith in poets who can go short.

Small poems are drastic examples of poetry's way of squeezing large content into tight spaces. Unlike haiku, the small poem has no rules except to be small. Its length, or lack of it, is its only formal requirement.

The small poem is a flash, a gesture, a gambit without the game that follows. There's no room for landscape here, or easeful reflection, but there is the opportunity for humor and poignancy. And this minimalist practice has its masters. Here's A. R. Ammons:

Their Sex Life

One failure on
Top of another.

And a forlorn one-liner by W. S. Merwin:

Elegy

Who would I show it to

Compared to the ocean liner of Milton's *Lycidas*, Merwin's single line is a canoe, but there it remains, untippable, floating on the lake of a page.

At some point, I began to think of the small poem as its own distinct form, and I started making my own little contributions to the genre.

Acknowledgments

Several of these poems have appeared in *Echo*, *Brilliant Corners*, and *Rolling Stone*. "Flaubert," "3:00 AM," and "Elegy" appeared in *The New Yorker*.

I'm indebted to the many people at Random House who helped bring this book into being, especially my remarkable editor, David Ebershoff, for his immediate belief in the value of these smallish poems. Thanks also to Mark Pigott for his lively friendship and support, and to Chris Calhoun, my agent and pal, who has long been in my corner. A greater debt is owed to my wife, Suzannah, who deserves my daily acknowledgment for loving me and for liking quite a few of these poems.

BILLY COLLINS is a former Poet Laureate of the United States. He is the author of twelve collections of poetry, including the bestsellers *Aimless Love, The Trouble with Poetry*, and *Sailing Alone Around the Room.* He is also the editor of *Poetry 180: A Turning Back to Poetry, 180 More: Extraordinary Poems for Every Day,* and *Bright Wings: An Illustrated Anthology of Poems About Birds.* A former Distinguished Professor at Lehman College of the City University of New York, Collins served as New York State Poet from 2004 to 2006. In 2016 he was inducted into the American Academy of Arts and Letters. He lives in Florida with his wife, Suzannah.

About the Type

The text of this book was set in Filosofia, a typeface designed in 1996 by Zuzana Licko, who created it for digital typesetting as an interpretation of the eighteenth-century typeface Bodoni, designed by Giambattista Bodoni (1740–1813). Filosofia, an example of Licko's unusual font designs, has classical proportions with a strong vertical feeling, softened by rounded droplike serifs. She has designed many typefaces and is the cofounder of *Emigre* magazine, where many of them first appeared. Born in Bratislava, Czechoslovakia, in 1961, Licko came to the United States in 1968. She studied graphic communications at the University of California, Berkeley, graduating in 1984.